Green Alert!

Contents

Written by Isabel Thomas

Collins

Green tricks

Trees have lush green crowns.
Shrubs have sweet-smelling flowers.
But do not be fooled!

Trees, shrubs and weeds have cunning tricks to avoid being munched!

Packed with poison

This bee slurps the nectar but keeps clear of the green parts. They are packed with poison.

The weed's bitter poisons stop cows from chomping them.

Some insects *can* munch toxic weeds!
This sort of cricket has adapted to crunch the weed without being harmed.

The scarlet seeds of this tree are toxic for us. But they do not harm starlings. Starlings love to swoop down and grab them.

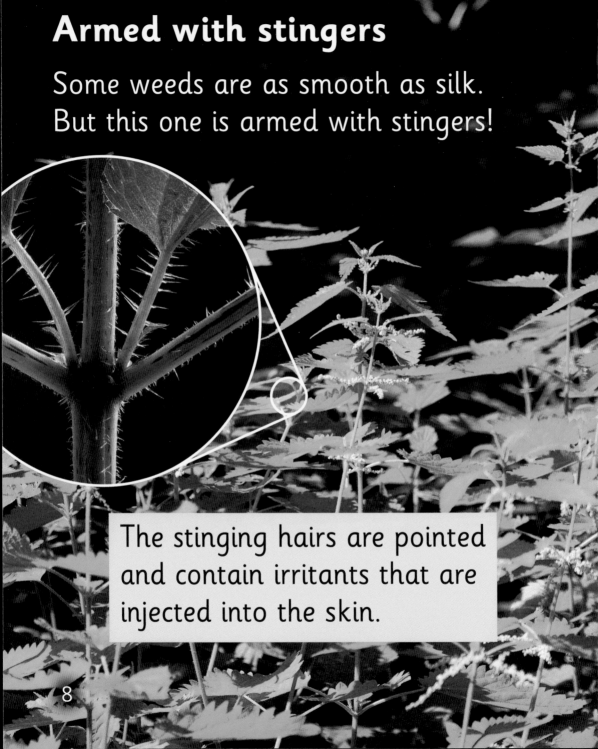

Armed with stingers

Some weeds are as smooth as silk.
But this one is armed with stingers!

The stinging hairs are pointed
and contain irritants that are
injected into the skin.

Stings help the weed defend itself.
Rabbits dislike being stung so they avoid
this weed.

Caterpillars like this are not bothered by the stings. They have sting-proof skin!

Moth eggs will not be disturbed here, thanks to the stings!

eggs

Pool of doom

This herb has a pool, but it's not for swimming! Insects land on the smooth part. Then they slip into the pool and drown.

This frog drinks from the pool without slipping. It might grab an insect snack too!

Croak!

Green alert!

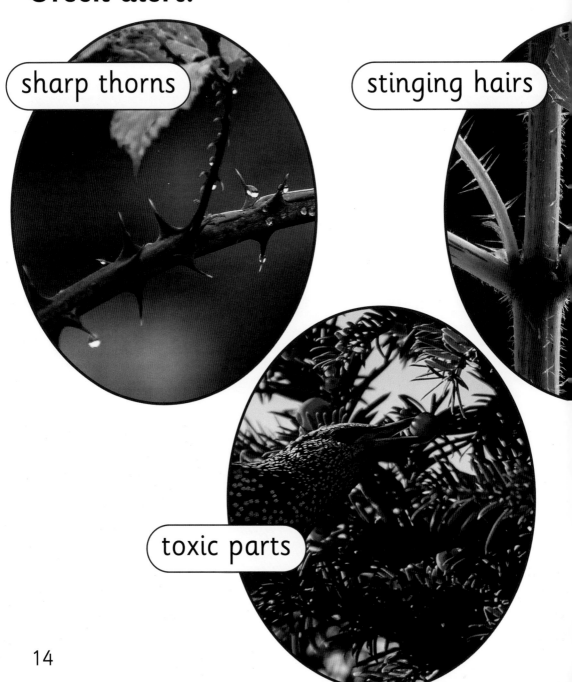

sharp thorns

stinging hairs

toxic parts

14

bitter poisons

pool

15

✿ Review: After reading ✿

Use your assessment from hearing the children read to choose any GPCs, words or tricky words that need additional practice.

Read 1: Decoding

- Remind the children to consider the context to work out the meaning of words, especially as words can have more than one meaning. Ask the children to work out the meaning of the following words in context:

  page 2 **crowns** (e.g. *tops*)   page 10 **proof** (e.g. *protected from*)

  page 12 **pool** (e.g. *small amount of water*)

- Ask the children to sound out these words to check they don't miss the adjacent consonants:

  d/i/s/t/ur/b/ed   f/l/ow/er/s   s/c/ar/l/e/t   s/m/oo/th

- Turn to pages 12 and 13 and challenge the children to take turns to read a sentence smoothly. Say: Can you sound out and blend any words you're unsure of in your head silently, before reading them aloud?

Read 2: Prosody

- Turn to page 6, and discuss why **can** is in italics. (*for emphasis*) Model reading the sentence, emphasising **can**.
- Ask: Which words are the most important in the next sentence? Model reading using their ideas. If necessary, suggest **Crickets** and **without**, to emphasise that the sentence is about how crickets of this sort are different.
- Encourage the children to experiment with which words to emphasise on page 7. (e.g. *emphasise: us, not, love*)

Read 3: Comprehension

- Ask the children what they already know about trees or flowers, and encourage them to describe their gardens or the plants they've seen in parks or woods.
- Ask the children what the main subject of this book is. If they suggest, for example, "plants" say: Yes, but what is special about most of the plants?
  o Return to the title, and discuss how all the plants might put animals on alert. (e.g. *they have clever ways of stopping things eating them*)
- Ask the children to find the pages and answers as fast as they can:
  o Which pages tell me about plants that sting? (*pages 8–11*)
     Why doesn't a caterpillar get stung? (*its skin is sting proof*)
  o Can you tell me what page tells me about poisonous plants? (*pages 4–7*)
     Do red berries poison starlings? (*no*)
- Turn to pages 14 and 15. Encourage the children to talk about how each plant defends itself.